DESSERT COOKBOOK FOR

BEGINNERS ADULT

From a Beginner to a Pro in only 20 Days. Start off Cooking by Preparing 23 Mouthwatering and Addictive Desserts for your Friends and Family

Table of Contents

INTRODUCTION

There's a motivation behind why your body wants certain heavenly desserts. Low carb diets frequently ignore the way that carbs are a fundamental supplement for the body. While desserts may not be the best type of starches, the correct guilty pleasures can fuel your body and brain.

Desserts make you more joyful

Have you at any point taken a chomp of your number one dessert and felt immediately shipped to a more elevated level of joy? That feeling is genuine.

As per The Nest, food varieties that have a normally high level of carbs help the mind and body produce synthetic compounds (like serotonin) that add to generally enthusiastic prosperity.

Enjoying your #1 dessert modifies your brain and body decidedly. Exploit this logical interaction by permitting yourself to enjoy your #1 sweet treat without that additional side of blame. You truly are benefiting your body!

Dessert recipes

1.   Bake well tart

Prep: 25 mins| Cook: 55 mins | Plus chilling | Easy|
Serves 8

Ingredients

- 250g plain flour, in addition to extra for carrying out
- ¼ tsp. fine ocean salt
- 2 tbsp. icing sugar
- 140g virus spread, cubed
- 2 egg yolks, beaten
- Cream or custard, to serve (discretionary)
- For the filling
- 100g salted spread, mollified
- 100g caster sugar
- 50g ground almonds

- 1 tsp. almond extricate
- 2 medium eggs, beaten
- 3 tbsp. raspberry jam
- 50g chipped almonds
- 80g icing sugar

Strategy

1. Heat the oven to 200C/180C fan/gas 6. To make the baked good, put the flour in a food processor alongside the salt and icing sugar. Rush to join. Add the margarine and heartbeat in short blasts until it's the surface of fine breadcrumbs. Blend 4 tbsp. cold water with the beaten eggs and shower into the combination, at that point rapidly heartbeat to consolidate. Tip out the brittle combination onto a work surface, at that point structure into a puck, cover and chill for 30 mins.

2. Carry the cake out on a delicately floured surface to around 25cm, and to the thickness of a £1 coin. Line a 20cm fluted tart tin with the baked good, leaving the cake to overhang. Add a large circle of preparing material large enough to cover the edges, and some heating beans to overload it (utilize dried rice or lentils

in the event that you don't have preparing beans).

3. Prepare for 15 mins, at that point eliminate the material and beans and heat for a further 7-10 mins or until the base is uniformly cooked. Trim off any overhanging cake with a serrated blade.

4. For the filling, beat the spread and sugar until consolidated. Add the ground almonds, almond concentrate and eggs and beat briefly. Spread the jam over the cake, at that point top with the almond filling. Dissipate over the chipped almonds and prepare for 25-30 mins until brilliant and firm. Leave to cool in the tin (or eat warm at this stage and leave out stage 4).

5. Combine as one the icing sugar and 1-2 tsp. water and shower over the tart. Cut and present with cream or custard, in the event that you like.

Formula TIPS

6. Step by step instructions to MAKE GREAT PASTRY

7. The way in to a rich, short cake is having freezing ingredients, ensure your margarine is

directly from the ice chest and that your water is super cold. Pour some water in to a container with some ice solid shapes prior to apportioning.

8. Works out in a good way for
9. Coconut, syrup and lime tart
10. Irish apple tart
11. Rum and coconut remedy tart

2. Easy cornflake tart

Prep: 20 mins| Cook: 40 mins| Easy| Serves 8-10

Ingredients

- 320g prepared moved short crust cake
- Plain flour, to clean
- 50g margarine
- 125g brilliant syrup
- 25g light brown delicate sugar
- 100g cornflakes
- 125g strawberry or raspberry jams
- Custard, to serve

Technique

1. Heat the oven to 180C/160C fan/gas 4. Unroll the cake and momentarily carry out on a softly floured work surface until its large enough to fit a 23cm free lined tart tin. Utilize the turning pin to lift the baked good ridiculous, at that point press into the corners and sides so the abundance cake looms over the edge. Cut this back, leaving simply a modest quantity of overabundance looming over the edge.

2. Line the baked good with heating material and load up with preparing beans or uncooked rice. Heat for 15 mins. Eliminate the material and beans, at that point heat for another 5-10 mins until simply brilliant. Eliminate from the oven and trim any overabundance cake from the edges using a serrated blade.

3. Heat the margarine, syrup and sugar in a little container with a touch of salt, blending regularly, until softened and smooth. Overlap in the cornflakes to cover in the spread blend.

4. Spoon the jam into the cooked cake base, at that point level the surface. Tip the cornflake blend over the jam and delicately push down until the entirety of the jam is covered with a layer of the combination. Return the tart to the oven and prepare for another 5 mins until the cornflakes are brilliant and toasted. Leave to cool until simply warm prior to cutting and presenting with custard.

3. Christmas sticky toffee pudding

Prep: 20 mins| Cook: 2 hrs. and 35 mins| Plus cooling| Easy| Serves 12

Ingredients

- 250g dates, pitted and finely chopped
- 100g raisins
- 200ml brilliant or spiced rum
- 150g spread, mollified, in addition to extra for the bowl
- 50g light muscovado sugar
- 3 large eggs, beaten
- 375g self-raising flour
- ½ tsp. blended flavor
- 1 tsp. ground cinnamon
- 50ml milk
- Vanilla custard or frozen yogurt, to serve
- For the toffee sauce
- 75g light muscovado sugar
- 2 tbsp. remedy
- 2 tbsp. brilliant syrup
- 75g spread

- 150ml twofold cream

Strategy

1. Put the dates, raisins, rum and 100ml water in a little pot and set over a low heat until steaming, around 5 mins (or do this in the microwave). Leave to cool.

2. In the interim, make the toffee sauce. Put every one of the ingredients aside from the cream in a little dish and bring to a stew. Cook until the sugar has broken up and the sauce is shiny, around 5 mins. Pour in the cream and cook for 2 mins more, mixing ceaselessly, at that point eliminate from the heat and put away. The sauce will keep on thickening as it cools.

3. Liberally margarine a 1.5-liter pudding bowl. Beat the spread and sugar until all around joined in a large bowl using an electric whisk, or in a stand blender. Add the eggs each in turn, beating great between every option. Crease in the flour, flavors and the splashed natural product until equally fused; at that point mix in the milk.

4. Pour a fourth of the toffee sauce into the base of the readied bowl, at that point spoon in the wipe player. Spot a sheet of preparing material over a sheet of foil, at that point make a crease in the middle. Utilize this to cover the pudding, material side down, and tie safely under the lip of the bowl using kitchen string.

5. Move the bowl to a liner. On the other hand, put an improved plate in the base of a large dish; sit the bowl on top, and half-fill the

container with water from the pot so it goes mostly up the side of the bowl. Cover and cook over a low heat for 2 hrs. 35 mins, checking the water level now and again and besting up when required.

6. Check the wipe is prepared by embedding's a stick into the center. In the event that it tells the truth, the wipe is cooked. In the event that any uncooked hitter sticks to the stick, keep steaming, check again after around 20 mins.

7. To serve, warm the excess toffee sauce over a low heat, reverse the wipe onto a serving plate, and pour over the warmed sauce. Present with custard or frozen yogurt.

8. Formula tip

9. You can make the pudding as long as seven days ahead of time. After it's steamed, eliminate the foil and preparing material and leave to cool totally. Stack a new sheet of preparing material over a new sheet of foil, crease, and use to cover the pudding as in the past. Keep the pudding in the refrigerator or a cool, evaporate place for to multi week. To serve, steam for 1 hr. until completely reheated. Cover the held sauce and keep in the cooler, at that point reheat completely over a low heat for around 5 mins prior to serving.

10. Figure out how to steam a pudding in our convenient guide.

11. Works out positively for

12. Mint chocolate chip treats

13. Brookies

14. Cold coconut portion cake

4. Tiramisu meringue roulade

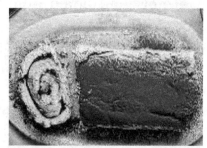

Prep: 40 mins| Cook: 20 mins| Easy| Serves 8 – 10

Ingredients

- For the meringue
- 4 large egg whites at room temperature
- 200g caster sugar
- Icing sugar and cocoa powder, for tidying
- For the mascarpone cream
- 200ml twofold cream
- 50g dim brown delicate sugar
- 150g mascarpone
- 3 tbsp. masala espresso alcohol or ordinary espresso alcohol (discretionary)
- For the espresso ganache
- 4 tbsp. moment espresso, disintegrated in 50ml bubbling water and left to cool marginally
- 100g dull chocolate, softened and left to cool somewhat

Strategy

1. To begin with, make the ganache. Whisk the espresso and liquefied chocolate together until you have a smooth, shiny blend. Leave to cool and thicken, blending periodically.

2. Heat the oven to 180C/160C fan/gas 4. Line a 23 x 32cm preparing plate with heating material. For the meringue, beat the egg whites and a touch of salt with an electric rush until hardened marginally.

3. Add 1 tbsp. of the caster sugar to the egg whites, at that point whisk again to solid pinnacles. Rehash with the remainder of the sugar, a spoonful at a time, until the combination is thick and gleaming. Spread equally into the plate, at that point heat for 15-20 mins, or until fresh to the touch and softly brilliant in places. Leave to cool totally.

4. For the mascarpone cream filling, put the cream, sugar, mascarpone and alcohol, if using, in a medium bowl and race until thickened.

5. To collect, filter some icing sugar over a large sheet of preparing material; at that point cautiously flip the cooled meringue onto it. Takeoff the tin and strip away the preparing material. With a short end confronting you, score a line 2cm into the edge of the meringue. Spread the ganache equitably absurd, at that point top with the cream, smoothing it with a range blade, at that point cautiously fold into a roulade, beginning from the scored end and using the material to help. Move to a serving plate and residue with cocoa powder.

6. Works out positively for

7. Apple and almond disintegrate pie

8. Peanut butter and jam pudding

9. Salted caramel and hazelnut banoffee pie

5. Self-saucing sticky toffee chocolate pudding

Prep: 20 min| Cook: 40 mins| Plus 30 mins soaking| Easy| Serves 8 – 10

Ingredients

- 200g pitted medjool dates
- 100g unsalted margarine, mellowed, in addition to extra for the dish
- 75g demerara sugar
- 75g dim brown delicate sugar
- 2 large eggs
- 250g plain flour
- 1 tsp. bicarbonate of pop
- 1 tbsp. heating powder
- 100g dim chocolate, generally chopped
- Vanilla frozen yogurt or custard, to serve
- For the sauce
- 200ml twofold cream
- 75g unsalted margarine, cubed
- 200g dull brown delicate sugar
- 30g cocoa powder

Technique

1. Put the dates in a bowl and pour in 300ml bubbling water. Leave to splash for 30 mins. In the mean time, make the sauce by tipping every one of the ingredients, a major spot of salt and 300ml bubbling water into a container, at that point speed over a medium heat and stew for 2 mins. Fill a container and leave to cool marginally. When the dates are drenched, utilize a hand blender to rush the dates and water until you have smooth paste. Leave to cool marginally. Spread a profound 35 x 25cm dish.

2. Heat oven to 180C/160C fan/gas 4. Beat together the spread and sugar for 3 mins until smooth. Add the eggs, each in turn, beating between every option. Overlay in the flour, bicarb and preparing powder alongside a spot of salt. When joined, blend in the date purée, at that point crease in obscurity chocolate. Empty the wipe hitter into the readied dish and spread out uniformly using the rear of a spoon. Pour the chocolate sauce equally over the highest point of the player.

3. Prepare in the oven for 30-35 mins until risen, at that point leave to rest for 2 mins. Serve warm with a major scoop of frozen yogurt or warm custard.

4. Works out positively for

5. The enormous twofold cheeseburger and mystery ingredient

6. Noodles with fresh stew oil eggs

7. Chicken arrabbiata stew and parmesan dumplings.

6. Lemon & elderflower celebration cake

Prep: 45 mins| Cook: 40 mins| More effort| Serves 15-18

Ingredients

- Oil, for lubing
- 6 medium eggs
- 100g common yogurt
- 50ml milk
- 450g spread, mellowed
- 450g brilliant caster sugar
- 450g self-raising flour
- Finely ground zing of 1 lemon, in addition to juice
- 3 tbsp. elderflower welcoming
- For the icing
- 250g spread, mellowed
- 300g full fat cream cheddar
- 700g icing sugar
- Finely ground zing of 1 lemon
- New blossoms to embellish

Technique

1. Heat oven to 160C/140C fan/gas 3. Oil and line the base and sides of 3 x 20cm cake tins with preparing material. In a container, whisk the eggs, yogurt and milk. Beat the spread and sugar together in a large bowl, using an electric hand whisk. At the point when you have a light and soft blend, add the flour, the fluid in the container and the lemon zing. Blend again until smooth. Split the cake combination between the tins, level the surfaces and prepare for 40 mins.

2. Blend the lemon juice and elderflower sincere. At the point when the cakes are cooked, jab everywhere on a superficial level with a mixed drink stick at that point spoon the lemon and elderflower syrup over the cakes. Leave to cool in the tins. When cool, you can envelop by stick film and save for 3 days prior to icing.

3. To make the icing, beat the margarine until smooth with an electric hand whisk. Add a large portion of the icing sugar, utilize a spatula to pound the blend together (this will assist with forestalling an icing sugar cloud) at that point whisk once more. Add the excess icing sugar, cream cheddar and lemon zing, crush once more, at that point whisk again until smooth.

4. Stack the cakes on a cake remain with a lot of icing between each layer. Heap the vast majority of the leftover good to beat all, utilization a range blade to spread it across the top and down the sides, covering the cake in whirls (don't stress over it looking excessively

awesome). Add the last piece of icing to the top and use it to cover any patches where the cake is jabbing through. Design with new blossoms.

7. Chocolate orange brownie tart

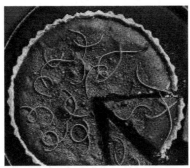

Prep: 20 mins| Cook: 1 hr.| Plus cooling| Easy
|Serves 6-8

Ingredients

- 320g pack instant short crust baked well
- 120g dim chocolate, chopped
- 120g margarine, cubed
- 2 eggs
- 80g brilliant caster sugar
- 80g light brown delicate sugar
- 80g plain flour
- 1 orange, zested and squeezed in addition to more zing to serve
- Crème fraîche to serve

Technique

1. Heat the oven to 180C/fan 160C/gas 4. Unwind the short crust baked good sheet and use to line a 20cm tart tin. Press into the sides of the tin and inexactly cut around the edges, leaving a little overhanging. Line the baked good with a scrunched-up piece of heating material, and load up with crude rice or

preparing beans. Prepare for 15 mins, eliminate the paper and heat for another 5-10 mins until dry.

2. While the cake is cooking, put the margarine and chocolate into a heatproof bowl set over a dish of just-stewing water and soften together, mixing frequently. At the point when liquefied, eliminate from the heat and leave to cool somewhat. Add a spot of salt if your margarine is unsalted.

3. Whisk together the eggs and sugars momentarily in a bowl until joined, at that point mix in the liquefied chocolate and spread. Strainer over the flour and overlap in until just consolidated. Mix in the squeezed orange and zing.

4. Trim the edges of the baked good tart with a serrated blade to neaten, and spoon the brownie blend into the center. Smooth over with the rear of a spoon or spatula, and prepare for a further 30-35 mins until the excellent conditions a hull, and the filling is not, at this point wet yet marginally flimsy.

5. Leave to cool for 15 mins prior to eliminating from the tin if serving warm, or serve at room temperature. Present with a bit of crème fraîche, and some more orange zing ground over. Saves for 3 days in an impenetrable compartment.

6. Works out positively for

7. Apple turnovers

8.   White chocolate & raspberry ripple baked cheesecake

Prep: 35 mins| Cook: 1 hr. and 35 mins| Plus 6 hrs.| chilling| More effort| Serves 10

Ingredients

- For the base
- 225g stomach related bread rolls
- 15g freeze-dried raspberries (discretionary)
- 115g margarine, liquefied
- For the filling
- 250g new or frozen raspberries
- ½ lemon, squeezed
- 175g caster sugar, in addition to 2 tsp.
- 600g full-fat delicate cheddar
- 3 large eggs, in addition to 2 egg yolks
- 175g twofold cream
- 1 tbsp. vanilla bean paste
- 350g white chocolate

Technique

1. Heat the oven to 180C/160C fan/gas 4, and line the base of a 23cm spring form cake tin with preparing material. Tip the bread rolls and freeze-dried raspberries, if using, into a food processor, and barrage to fine scraps. Heartbeat in the spread to cover the scraps, at that point tip the combination into the readied tin and press into an even layer using the rear of a spoon. Chill until required.

2. For the filling, put the raspberries, lemon juice and 2 tsp. caster sugar in a dish over a medium heat. Cook for 4-5 mins until the berries have mollified and get delicious. Move to a food processor and rush until smooth. Tip into a bowl and leave to cool. On the off chance that you incline toward a smooth purée, strainer the combination through a fine cross section sifter and dispose of the pips.

3. Beat the delicate cheddar using an electric rush until relaxed, at that point race in 175g sugar, the eggs, yolks, cream and vanilla until smooth. Liquefy the white chocolate in a heatproof bowl in the microwave in 20-second blasts, or over a dish of stewing water, guaranteeing the lower part of the bowl doesn't contact the water. Slowly pour 33% of the improved delicate cheddar combination into the dissolved chocolate, whisking persistently until consolidated, at that point empty that into the remainder of the delicate cheddar blend. Speed until completely consolidated.

4. Eliminate the tin from the ice chest, and firmly wrap the lower part of the tin with foil to forestall any spilling. Sit the tin in a profound broiling tin. Pour the cheesecake blend over the roll base. Spoon over the raspberry purée, and twirl it into the cheesecake blend using a stick.

5. Put the broiling tin in the oven, at that point empty sufficient boiling water into the simmering tin to come 2½ cm up the side of the cake tin. Prepare for 1 hr. 15 mins-1 hr. 30 mins, or until the edge of the cheesecake is set, however the middle has a slight wobble (it will keep on setting in the cooler).

6. Put the tin on a wire rack, at that point run a little, sharp blade around the edge. Leave to cool totally in the tin, at that point chill for at any rate 6 hrs. prior to eliminating from the tin.

7. Works out positively for

8. Smoked salmon pâté with tear and offer brioche buns

9. Curried spread prepared cod with cauliflower and chickpeas

10. Coconut French toast with spiced cooked pineapple.

9. Easy banoffee pie

Prep: 25 mins| Plus chilling| Easy| Serves 8-10

Ingredients

- 225g stomach related rolls
- 150g spread, liquefied
- 397g can caramel or 400g dulce de leche
- 3 little bananas cut
- 300ml twofold cream
- 1 tbsp. icing sugar
- 1 square dull chocolate (discretionary)

Strategy

1. Smash the stomach related bread rolls, either by hand using a wooden spoon, or in a food processor, until you get fine morsels, tip into a bowl. Blend the squashed bread rolls in with the liquefied margarine until completely joined. Tip the combination into a 23cm free lined fluted tart tin and cover the tin, including the sides, with the roll in an even layer. Push down

with the rear of a spoon to smooth the surface and chill for 1 hr., or overnight.

2. Beat the caramel to slacken and spoon it over the lower part of the bread roll base. Spread it out equally using the rear of a spoon or range blade. Tenderly drive the chopped banana into the highest point of the caramel until the base is covered. Put in the refrigerator.

3. Whip the cream with the icing sugar until surging and thick. Remove the pie from the refrigerator and spoon the whipped cream on top of the bananas. Mesh the dim chocolate over the cream, in the event that you like, and serve.

10. Victoria sponge loaf cake

Prep: 35 mins| Cook: 1 hr.| Plus cooling| Easy |
Serves 8-10

Ingredients
- Sunflower or vegetable oil, for the tin
- 200g spread, mollified
- 200g caster sugar
- 4 medium eggs, beaten
- 200g self-rising flour
- 2 tbsp. milk
- 1 tsp. vanilla concentrate
- 400g strawberries
- 50g icing sugar
- 200g strawberry jam
- ½ lemon, squeezed
- 200ml twofold cream

Technique
1. Oil a 950g portion tin (our own deliberate 19 x 9cm across the base) and line with a segment of heating material, leaving a little looming over the edges – this will help you lift the cake

out later. Heat the oven to 170C/150C fan/gas 3.

2. Put the margarine and caster sugar in a large bowl, or stand blender. Beat together using an electric whisk or the blender until pale and cushy – this will require a couple of moments.

3. Progressively add the egg, a little at an at once, between every option until the combination is smooth. Add a tablespoon or two of the flour if it's beginning to sour.

4. Add the excess flour, the milk and vanilla, and blend until there are no noticeable dashes of flour. Scratch into the readied tin, at that point utilize a spatula to equitably spread it and smooth the surface. Heat on the center rack of the oven for 50 mins-1 hr., or until a stick embedded into the center confesses all. On the off chance that any wet cake blend sticks to the stick, prepare for 5 mins more, at that point check once more. Leave to cool in the tin for 10 mins, at that point cautiously move to a wire rack and leave to cool totally.

5. Slash four of the strawberries into little pieces and blend in with 1 tsp. of the icing sugar. Put away. Divide or quarter a portion of the leftover strawberries and leave the rest entirety. Blend the excess icing sugar with 2 tsp. of the jam and all the lemon juice to make a thick icing – it ought to be adequately thick to shower down the sides of the cake. Empty the cream into a bowl and speed until it's simply holding its shape – be mindful so as not to over whisk, as it will keep on thickening as

you pipe it. Move the cream to a funneling pack fitted with a fine star spout.

6. Cut the cake into equal parts lengthways through the center using a sharp serrated blade. Spread a tad bit of the leftover jam over the base layer. Line a large portion of the whipped cream over in a crisscross example and top with the chopped strawberries and any sweet squeeze from the bowl. Sandwich with the highest point of the cake. Line the excess whipped cream over similarly, at that point orchestrates the split, quartered and entire strawberries on top. Sprinkle over the icing to wrap up. Best served that very day, yet will save canvassed in the refrigerator for as long as three days.

7. Works out in a good way for

8. Pear, hazelnut and chocolate cake

9. Lemon wipes cake

10. Rhubarb and custard sandwich bread rolls

11. Banana tray bake with cream cheese frosting

Prep: 30 mins| Cook: 40 mins| Plus cooling| Easy|
Makes 20 squares

Ingredients

- 200g brilliant caster sugar
- 300g ready bananas (2 medium), stripped
- 125ml flavorless oil like sunflower or grape seed
- 4 eggs
- 125g whole meal or rye flour
- 100g plain flour
- 1 tsp. cinnamon
- 3 tsp. heating powder
- 100g white chocolate chips or chopped pecans (discretionary)
- Icing
- 100g unsalted margarine, mollified
- 100g icing sugar, sieved
- 200g full-fat cream cheddar
- Large squeeze cinnamon

Technique

1. Line a 25 x 20cm tray bake tin with preparing material and heat the oven to 190C/170C fan/gas 5. Tip the sugar, bananas, oil and eggs into a large bowl and whisk them together. Assuming your bananas are ready, you can utilize an inflatable rush for this, or utilize a fork to crush. Add the flours, cinnamon and preparing powder and whisk the combination until everything is simply joined – don't take too long over this piece as the heating powder will have begun to actuate. Mix in the chocolate chips, if using, and scoop the blend into your tin. Heat for 30-40 mins or until the wipe is firm and springy to the touch and daintily browned on top. Cool in the tin.

2. To make the icing, beat the margarine until it is truly delicate at that point beat in the icing sugar. Utilize a spatula to crease in the delicate cheddar, ensuring it is all altogether blended in. Try not to be enticed to beat the blend, this will make it runnier.

3. Lift the cake cautiously out of the tin, strip off the paper and move it to a plate or board. Spread over the icing, making it as slick or chaotic as you prefer. Daintily dust the top with cinnamon – utilize a tea sifter to assist with this on the off chance that you have one. Slice into pieces to serve. Will keep for as long as 3 days in an impenetrable holder.

4. Works out in a good way For

5. Simple gooey brownies

6. Delicate gingerbread

12. Chocolate & salted caramel waffle bread & butter pudding

Prep: 20 mins| Cook: 30 mins| Plus at least 1 hr.| soaking| Easy| Serves 8

Ingredients

- 150g dull chocolate (in any event 70% cocoa solids)
- 300ml twofold cream
- 200ml milk
- 50g spread
- 1 tbsp. caster sugar
- Touch of ground cinnamon
- 1 tsp. vanilla concentrate
- 200g canned caramel or dulce de leche
- 10 cooked waffles (we utilized toaster oven waffles)
- 4 medium egg yolks, beaten (freeze the whites for another formula)
- Icing sugar, for cleaning (discretionary)

Strategy

1. Fill a large dish with a couple of centimeters of water and set over a medium heat. Set a large heatproof bowl over the skillet – it ought to sit on top without contacting the water. Break the chocolate into the bowl, at that point tip in the cream, milk, spread, caster sugar, cinnamon and vanilla. Diminish the heat to low, and mix the blend until everything has liquefied together and is shiny. Eliminate from the heat and leave to cool marginally.

2. Spread the caramel over the base of a preparing dish (our own was 30 x 22cm), at that point sprinkle with a spot of ocean salt. Slice the waffles down the middle corner to corner, at that point organize over the caramel in covering lines.

3. Empty the egg yolks into the warm chocolate blend, blending admirably as you do until the entirety of the egg is completely fused. Cautiously pour the chocolate custard over the waffles, guaranteeing they're completely covered. Leave to douse for at any rate 1 hr., or cover and chill for the time being.

4. Heat the oven to 180C/160C fan/gas 4 and uncover the dish in the event that it has been chilled. Heat the pudding for 30 mins until the custard is set with a slight wobble in the middle. Leave to represent 5 mins, at that point dust daintily with icing sugar, on the off chance that you like, and scoop into bowls to serve.

5. Formula tip

6. Use bread all things being equal

7. You can trade the toaster oven waffles for white bread. For the best outcomes, utilize a portion that is a couple of days old. In the event that using bread instead of waffles, you'll need to improve the custard with 50g caster sugar.

13. Baked vegan cheesecake with raspberries & clementine

Prep: 25 mins| Cook: 1 hr. and 30 mins| Plus 1 hr. soaking and at least 3 hrs. chilling |More effort| Serves 8

Ingredients

- 100g unsalted cashews
- 175g coconut cream
- 150g vegetarian delicate cheddar
- 1 tbsp. corn flour
- 2 tsp. vanilla bean paste
- 70ml maple syrup
- 50g coconut oil, softened
- ½ lemon, squeezed
- 200g raspberries
- 2 tbsp. caster sugar
- 50g shelled pistachios, generally chopped
- 50g sugar coated clementine strip
- For the base
- 200g porridge oats
- 75g caster sugar
- 4 tbsp. coconut oil, softened

Technique

1. Put the cashews in a large heatproof bowl and cover with bubbling water from the pot. Leave to mollify for 1 hr.
2. Heat the oven to 200C/180C fan/gas 6. Line the base of a 20cm (4cm profound) round cake tin with preparing material. To make the base, put the oats, sugar and a spot of salt in a food processor and barrage to a fine powder. Heartbeat in the coconut oil until consolidated, at that point bit by bit beat in 3-4 tbsp. water until it meets up into a batter – it ought to be brittle, not tacky.
3. Press the mixture into the base and up the side of the tin using the rear of a spoon. Prepare for 20-25 mins until brilliant. Leave to cool.
4. Lessen the oven to 180C/160C fan/gas 4. Channel the cashews; at that point move to a blender alongside the coconut cream, delicate cheddar, corn flour, vanilla, maple syrup, coconut oil, lemon juice and a spot of salt. Barrage on fast until the blend is velvety and smooth.
5. Pour the cashew and delicate cheddar combination over the base and heat for 1 hr-1 hr. 15 mins until the edge is simply shaded and the middle has for the most part set with simply a slight wobble. Leave to cool totally (it will sink somewhat as it cools), at that point chill for at any rate 3 hrs. or overnight.
6. Stage 6
7. Put the raspberries and sugar in a heatproof bowl and microwave for 1 min 30 seconds on high. Mix and leave to cool totally, at that point

pour this ludicrous. Dissipate over the pistachios and candy-coated clementine strip. Will keep chilled for as long as three days.

8. Works out positively For
9. Chocolate and peanut butter Pavlova
10. Mojito possets
11. Dark Forest ice chest cake

14. Strawberry tart

Prep: 35 mins| Cook: 45 mins+ Chilling| Easy|
Serves 12

Ingredients

- 125g unsalted spread, mollified somewhat
- 85g icing sugar
- 1 egg
- 200g plain flour, in addition to extra for cleaning
- 100g strawberry jam
- 500g strawberries, (little hulled, large cut)
- 2 tbsp. apricot jam
- For the crème pâtissière
- 300ml milk
- 150ml twofold cream
- 1 tsp. vanilla concentrate
- 3 egg yolks
- 60g caster sugar
- 3½ tbsp. corn flour
- 50g spread, cubed and mollified

Strategy

1. Beat the spread and sugar together until smooth, yet not soft. Blend in the egg until consolidated; at that point add the flour. Unite with your hands to frame a mixture. Wrap and chill in the ice chest for 30 mins.

2. Residue a surface with flour and carry out the cake to a 26cm circle (or 3cm greater than your tin). Line a 23cm fluted tart tin with the baked good, leaving a shade. Prick the base with a fork to stop any air bubbles framing. Chill for 30 mins.

3. Heat the oven to 200C/180C fan/gas 6. Line the cake case with a scrunched up sheet of preparing material and heating beans, at that point prepare for 15 mins. Eliminate the material and beans and heat for 15-20 mins more until fresh and brilliant. Leave in the tin to cool.

4. To make the crème pâtissière, heat the milk, cream and vanilla in a skillet over a medium heat, blending sometimes. Rise to a stew. In the mean time, whisk the yolks and sugar in a bowl for 3 mins until pale, at that point mix in the corn flour until consolidated. Pour a fourth of the hot cream over the egg blend, whisking persistently, at that point empty the warm egg blend into the dish with the remainder of the cream. Mix over a low-medium heat for 5-8 mins until the crème pâtissière thickens. Move to a large bowl and cool for 15 mins, whisking incidentally. Slowly race in the margarine until smooth, cover and put in the ice chest until required.

5. Beat the strawberry jam to release it, at that point spread over the lower part of the cake case. Put the crème pâtissière into a funneling sack and line in a twisting on top of the jam. Organize the strawberries on top in an example. Heat the apricot jam in a little dish with 1 tbsp. water until warm. Race to release the jam, at that point leave to cool marginally. Brush over the highest point of the strawberries.

15. Dark chocolate & passion fruit tart

Prep: 1 hr. and 15 mins| Cook: 50 mins| Plus 6 hrs.30 mins chilling | More effort| Serves 10

Ingredients

- 180g plain flour, in addition to extra for cleaning
- 85g icing sugar
- 50g cocoa powder, in addition to 1-2 tbsp. for tidying
- 140g cold unsalted spread, cut into blocks
- 2 egg yolks
- Cocoa nibs, to enhance (discretionary)
- Crème fraîche, to serve
- For the energy organic product curd
- 200g enthusiasm natural product mash (from around 8-10 energy organic products)
- 1 leaf gelatine
- 3 medium eggs
- 70g unsalted margarine
- 50g caster sugar
- 1½ tbsp. corn flour

- For the dim chocolate ganache
- 150g dim chocolate (in any event 70% cocoa solids)
- 150ml twofold cream
- 150g light brown delicate sugar

Technique

1. Filter the flour, icing sugar, cocoa and ½ tsp. salt into a bowl. Focus on the margarine with your fingers until the combination looks like breadcrumbs. Add the egg yolks alongside 2 tbsp. super cold water, and keep on blending in with your hands until a delicate batter structures. Then again, beat the ingredients together in a food processor. Wrap the batter and chill for at any rate 1 hr. Will keep chilled for as long as two days.
2. Line the base of a 23cm free lined tart tin with heating material. Carry the batter out on a daintily floured surface to the thickness of a £1 coin, at that point use it to line the tart tin, squeezing it up the side and leaving some overhanging. Cover and chill for another 1 hr.
3. Heat the oven to 190C/170C fan/gas 5. Line the baked good with preparing material and load up with heating beans. Heat for 20 mins. Eliminate the beans and material and heat for 20 mins more until fresh. Leave to cool totally, at that point utilize a sharp blade to manage the abundance cake.
4. To make the curd, put the energy natural product mash in a food processor and barrage to isolate the seeds and tissue. Push through a strainer over a medium pot; at that point

dispose of the seeds. Tip in the excess ingredients and set the dish over a low heat. Speed until the margarine has liquefied, at that point, using a wooden spoon, mix until the curd has thickened, around 10 mins. (Try not to turn up the heat to accelerate the cycle, as the eggs will coagulate.) Stir well, particularly at the edge, as this is the place where the curd can get. Strainer into a bowl, leave to cool, at that point spoon into the case. Chill the filled tart for 30 mins.

5. To make the ganache, liquefy the chocolate, cream, sugar and a spot of ocean salt in a heatproof bowl over a container of stewing water, ensuring the bowl doesn't contact the water, blending until lustrous and thick. Eliminate from the heat, leave to cool for 15 mins, at that point pour over the curd layer. Dissipate over the cocoa nibs, on the off chance that using, chill for in any event 4 hrs. or overnight. Residue with cocoa at that point cut and present with crème fraîche.

6. Works out in a good way for

7. Apple and custard rose tart

8. Beetroot roti with green yogurt and smoked salmon

9. Fresh za'atar chicken pilaf with pomegranate

16. White chocolate, mascarpone & pistachio cheesecake

Prep: 30 mins| Cook: 50 mins| Plus resting and cooling| More effort|Serves 12

Ingredients
- Spread, for the tin
- 100g white chocolate
- 200g stomach related rolls, squashed
- For the cake
- 500g mascarpone
- 200g full-fat yogurt
- 3 eggs
- 100g caster sugar
- 1 lemon, zested, 1/2 squeezed
- ½ tsp. vanilla bean paste
- 50g shelled pistachios, generally chopped
- 1 tbsp. icing sugar (discretionary)

- Blended berries, to serve (discretionary)

Strategy

1. Line the base of a profound 20cm spring form cake tin with preparing material and margarine the base and sides. Liquefy the white chocolate in a large heatproof bowl set over a dish of simply stewing water (guarantee the lower part of the bowl doesn't contact the water). On the other hand, liquefy the chocolate in a microwave in short blasts. At the point when the chocolate is totally smooth, mix in the bread rolls and a little spot of salt. Press into the base of the tin, right to the edges, guaranteeing the base is even. Put in the refrigerator to chill for in any event 20 mins.

2. Heat the oven to 140C/120C fan/gas 1. Beat the mascarpone, yogurt, eggs, caster sugar, lemon zing and juice and vanilla bean paste along with an electric speed until smooth, at that point tip over the bread roll base. Move the tin to a preparing plate and heat for 45 mins until practically set, with simply a slight wobble in the center. Turn the oven off with the cheesecake inside, and leave the entryway partially open. Leave the cheesecake to cool totally.

3. When totally cool and set, extricate the sides and base of the tin with a blade, and cautiously move the cheesecake to a serving plate. Disperse over the pistachios and residue with the icing sugar, at that point present with the berries as an afterthought.

4. Works out in a good way for

5. Cheesecake bombe with summer organic products
6. Custom made BBQ sheep doner kebab
7. Frozen banana and peanut butter cheesecake

17. Chocolate & marmalade steamed pudding with marmalade cream

Prep: 25 mins| Cook: 2 hrs. and 15 mins| More effort| Serves 8

Ingredients

- 175g margarine, in addition to extra for the bowl
- 45g cocoa powder
- 175g plain flour
- ¼ tsp. bicarbonate of pop
- 1 tsp. heating powder
- 200g light brown delicate sugar
- 1 orange, zested
- 3 large eggs, softly beaten
- 115g delicate set preserves, beaten to release
- 100g dim chocolate, chopped
- For the cream
- 300ml twofold cream
- 1 stored tbsp. icing sugar

- 125g delicate set preserves, beaten to release, in addition to extra to serve

Technique

1. Margarine a 1.2-liter pudding bowl and put a circle of buttered preparing material in the base.

2. Filter together the cocoa, flour, bicarb, heating powder and a touch of salt. Beat the spread and sugar together in an electric blender until pale and fleecy; at that point add the orange zing. Bit by bit add the eggs, a little at an at once, after every option. Mix in the preserves. Overlay in the filtered ingredients followed by the dull chocolate pieces. Scratch the player into the readied pudding bowl.

3. Put a piece of heating material on top of a sheet of foil (both ought to be adequately large to cover the bowl and shade the edges). Overlap a crease along the center; at that point place this, material side down, onto the pudding. The crease should stumble into the middle. Bind to the bowl solidly with string, using it to make a handle. Trim off the abundance material and foil.

4. Put the pudding in a large pot on a trivet or improved saucer. Add sufficient bubbling water to come 33% of the route up the sides of the bowl. Carry the water to the bubble, go down to a stew, cover the dish and steam the pudding for 2 hrs-2 hrs. 15 mins. Keep beating up with heated water.

5. Lift the pudding out of the skillet, leave to sit for 10 mins, at that point run a blade between

the bowl and the edge of the pudding. Alter onto a plate – the pudding should slide out. Eliminate the material.

6. Whip the cream and icing sugar to delicate pinnacles; at that point mix in the jelly. Serve the pudding with a bit of the cream and some preserves on top.

18. Triple chocolate & peanut butter layer cake

Prep: 45 mins| Cook: 30 mins - 1 hr.| Plus cooling and 1 hr. 40 mins chilling| More effort| Serves 14

Ingredients

- 225ml rapeseed oil, in addition to additional for the tins
- 250g self-rising flour
- 4 tbsp. cocoa
- 1 ½ tsp. bicarbonate of pop
- 225g caster sugar
- 3 tbsp. brilliant syrup
- 3 large eggs, beaten
- 225ml milk
- For the pretzel bark
- 200g dull chocolate, chopped
- 2 tbsp. chocolate chips
- Little small bunch pretzel pieces
- 2 tbsp. honeycomb pieces
- For the icing
- 65g dull chocolate
- 250g delicate salted spread
- 500g icing sugar

- 45g smooth peanut butter
- 1-2 tbsp. cocoa
- For the ganache dribble
- 200ml twofold cream
- 100g dull chocolate, finely chopped
- For the beautification
- Chocolate eggs, some empty, some filled, gold brilliance, toffee popcorn and pretzels

Strategy

1. Heat oven to 180C/160C fan/gas 4. Oil and line the base of three 19cm sandwich tins. Blend the flour, cocoa, bicarb and sugar in a bowl. Make a well in the middle and beat in the syrup, eggs, oil and milk with an electric speed until smooth.

2. Split the blend between the tins, and prepare for 25-30 mins until the cakes are raised and firm to the touch. Cool in the tins for 10 mins prior to turning out onto a cooling rack and cooling totally. At this stage, they can be frozen, all around wrapped, for as long as about two months.

3. Make the bark while the cake is cooling. Liquefy the chocolate in short barges in the microwave, mixing each 20 secs, until smooth. Spoon onto a material fixed preparing plate and smooth over with a spatula to make a thinnish layer, around 35 x 20cm. Sprinkle over the chocolate chips alongside the bits of pretzel and honeycomb, at that point chill until strong. Eliminate the bark from the cooler and leave briefly to come to room temperature prior to using a sharp blade to cut it into

shards (if its refrigerator chilly, the chocolate will snap instead of cut). Chill again until you're prepared to design the cake.

4. To make the icing, dissolve the chocolate in the microwave, mixing between short impacts; at that point leave to cool a bit. Then, beat the margarine, icing sugar and 1 tbsp. bubbling water with an electric whisk or stand blender, slowly from the outset, at that point turn up the speed and beat until you get a pale, cushioned icing. Spoon out 33% of the blend into a different bowl and mix in the peanut butter. Whisk the dissolved chocolate into the rest of the icing, at that point beat in the cocoa on the off chance that you need a hazier, more chocolatey-shaded icing.

5. Sandwich the three cakes along with the peanut butter icing. Utilize a large portion of the chocolate icing to cover the sides and top of the cake and fill in the edges between the layers, scratching off any abundance. Chill for 20 mins. This is known as a scrap covering, permitting you to get a truly smooth completion with regards to the last icing.

6. Spread the leftover chocolate icing over the daintily chilled cake, streamlining the sides and top so you get a slick completion. Chill again for 20 mins.

7. To make the ganache, heat the cream in a little skillet until steaming. Tip the dull chocolate into a bowl; at that point pour over the cream. Blend well until smooth and sparkling. Move to a funneling pack and leave

to cool for a couple of mins at room temperature.

8. Line the ganache on top of the cake, bumping it over the edge and permitting it to dribble down flawlessly. Does this right round the cake, at that point fill in the middle with more ganache. Smooth the top with a blade. Chill for 1 hr. for the ganache to set.

9. Press the bark shards into the cake, standing up. Add heaps of chocolate eggs, popcorn and pretzels in and around the shards. Slice into cuts to serve. Will keep for as long as three days kept in a cool spot in an impermeable compartment.

10. Formula TIPS

11. Preparing IN BATCHES

12. In the event that you don't have three cake tins, prepare the wipes in clumps, cleaning and drying the tin in the middle of every one. You can utilize a 18cm tin in the event that you don't have 19cm tins; simply heat each cake for 5 mins more.

13. Works out positively For

14. Easter egg treats

15. Simnel portion cake

16. Hot cross cinnamon buns

19. White forest meringue roulade

Prep: 35 mins | Cook: 25 mins| More effort| Serves 8

Ingredients

- Margarine, for the tin
- 100g white chocolate, 50g ground, 50g liquefied and cooled a little
- For the meringue
- 4 large egg whites
- 1 tsp. lemon juice
- 200g white caster sugar
- Icing sugar, for tidying
- For the cherry filling
- 300g frozen dark cherries, saving a couple of entire ones to embellish
- 50ml squeezed orange
- 100g white caster sugar
- Spot of ground cloves
- ½ tsp. corn flour
- For the cream filling
- 400ml twofold cream
- 50g icing sugar

- ½ tsp. vanilla bean paste or concentrate

Technique

1. Heat oven to 180C/160C fan/gas 4. Margarine, at that point line a 23 x 32cm heating plate. Using an electric hand whisk beat the egg whites, lemon juice and a touch of salt until solid.

2. Add 1 tbsp. of the caster sugar; at that point rush until the combination makes firm pinnacles. Rehash with the remainder of the sugar, spoon by spoon, until the blend is thick and sparkly. Spread into the tin, at that point prepare for 15 mins or until fresh to the touch and gently brilliant in places. Leave to cool.

3. Stew the cherries, squeezed orange, sugar and cloves for 10 mins, or until the cherries are delicate yet at the same time holding their shape. Blend the corn flour in with 2-3 tsp. cold water to make a paste, mix into the cherries and cook a few mins more until the juices thicken. Leave to cool.

4. To amass, filter icing sugar over a large part of material, at that point cautiously flip the meringue onto it. Eliminate the tin and material. With a short end confronting you, score a line 2cm into the meringue.

5. Whip the cream, icing sugar and vanilla until thick yet not solid, at that point spread over the meringue. Spoon over about portion of the cherry sauce and disperse with the ground chocolate. Move up the roulade, beginning with the scored short end and using the paper under to help. Freeze the roulade for as long

as a month at that point thaws out for the time being. Freeze by setting on a material lined plate at that point, when firm, fold the material over it and cover with stick film. Freeze the leftover cherry sauce for as long as a month.

6. To serve, sprinkle with the softened white chocolate. Top with a couple of the entire cherries and serve the excess sauce as an afterthought.
7. Works out in a good way for
8. Rough street cheesecake pudding
9. Coconut custard tart with broiled pineapple
10.   Irish cream tiramisu

20. Flourless brownies

Prep: 20 mins| Cook: 30 mins| Easy Cuts into 16

Ingredients

- 200g spread, chopped, in addition to extra for the tin
- 250g dull chocolate (in any event 70% cocoa solids), broken into little pieces
- 225g caster sugar
- 3 eggs
- 100g ground almonds

Strategy

1. Heat the oven to 180C/160C fan/gas 4. Spread a 4cm-profound, 20 x 20cm square cake tin and line with preparing material. Soften 200g of the chocolate along with the margarine in a large heatproof bowl set over a dish of simply stewing water (guarantee the lower part of the bowl doesn't contact the water), blending incidentally. Eliminate from the heat and leave to cool for 10 mins.

2. In the mean time, whisk the sugar, eggs and a touch of salt together in a large bowl until pale

and frothy – it should resemble a foamy milkshake. This will take 2-3 mins with an electric whisk, or around 5-8 mins with an inflatable whisk. Pour in the spread and chocolate blend alongside the almonds; at that point crease everything together until there are no dashes of chocolate. Tip the combination into the tin, disperse over the remainder of the chocolate, and prepare for 25 mins, until cooked with a slight wobble in the center.

3. Leave to cool for 10 mins, at that point scoop into bowls and serve warm for a pudding. Then again, leave to cool totally in the tin, at that point cut into squares and store in an impermeable tin. Will keep for as long as five days.

21. Mojito cake

Prep: 25 mins | Cook: 40 mins| Plus infusing| More effort | Serves 10-12

Ingredients

- 225g salted spread, mellowed, in addition to extra for the tins
- 225g brilliant caster sugar
- 4 large eggs
- 225g self-rising flour
- 2 limes zing finely ground
- 50g characteristic yogurt
- Lime wedges, lime zing and mint leaves, to brighten
- For the syrup
- 3 limes, squeezed (90ml)
- 100g light brown delicate sugar
- Little pack mint leaves picked and generally chopped
- 120ml white rum
- For the buttercream
- 150g unsalted spread, mollified
- 400g icing sugar, sieved
- 2 limes, zested

- 50g cream cheddar

Strategy

1. Heat the oven to 180C/160C fan/gas 4. Spread and line two free lined 20cm round cake tins.
2. Put the spread and sugar in a large blending bowl. Beat for 5 mins with an electric speed until pale and cushy. Speed in the eggs each in turn, at that point overlay through the flour, ground lime zing and yogurt. Split the player between the readied tins and heat in the focal point of the oven for 25-30 mins, or until a stick embedded in the center confesses all. Leave in the tins for a min; at that point turn out onto wire racks.
3. To make the syrup, put a large portion of the lime juice and all the sugar and mint leaves into a pot and bring to a stew, adding 1 tbsp. water if necessary to break down the sugar. Delicately bubble for 7-10 mins, or until sweet. Eliminate from the heat and mix through the rum and remaining lime juice. Leave to imbue for 10 mins, at that point strain into a bowl.
4. Prick the warm cakes done with a mixed drink stick and pour over the syrup. Leave to cool totally.
5. To make the buttercream, put the margarine, icing sugar and lime zing in a bowl and beat with an electric speed for 5 mins until light and cushy. Beat in the cream cheddar until just consolidated, being mindful so as not to overbeat.
6. Put one of the syrup-doused wipes on a large serving plate and spoon more than 33% of the

buttercream, spreading it over with a range blade. Top with the other wipe and spread the leftover icing over the top and sides of the cake. Finish with the lime wedges, lime zing and mint leaves. Will keep in the cooler for as long as three days.

22. Speculoos profiterole wreath

Preparation and cooking time |Prep: 40 mins| Cook: 45 mins| More effort| Serves 6

Ingredients
- 100g plain flour
- 85g unsalted margarine
- 3 eggs, at room temperature
- 4-5 speculums rolls, disintegrated
- Gold sprinkles, to enrich (discretionary)
- For the filling
- 400ml twofold cream
- 250g speculoos bread roll spread
- ½ tsp. ground cinnamon
- 1 tsp. blended zest
- Grinding of nutmeg
- For the caramel sauce
- 130g granulated sugar
- 20g unsalted margarine
- 6 tbsp. twofold cream

- 1 tsp. vanilla bean paste
- ¼ tsp. ground cinnamon
- ¼ tsp. blended flavor

Technique

1. Strainer the flour and ¼ tsp. salt into a bowl. Carry the margarine and 225ml water to the bubble in a pan; at that point stew until the spread has dissolved. Tip in the flour combination and immediately beat with a wooden spoon until everything meets up into a smooth, sparkling batter that pulls from the side of the container. Tip the batter into a spotless bowl, and spread it up the side with the spoon to help it rapidly cool down a tore into (you don't need it to cool totally – it's simpler to join the eggs while it's still somewhat warm). Heat the oven to 200C/180C fan/gas 6 and line two preparing sheets with preparing material. Put away.

2. While the mixture is still marginally warm, break in the eggs each in turn, beating admirably with the wooden spoon between every expansion until smooth (you shouldn't utilize every one of the eggs). At the point when prepared, the batter ought to slowly tumble off the spoon in a V-shape – if the combination is excessively runny, you will not have the option to pipe it; if it's excessively thick, it will not puff up in the oven. Spoon the mixture into a channeling sack and cut off the end so it has a 1cm opening.

3. Holding the funneling pack at a 90-degree point to the heating plate, pipe pecan

measured chunks of batter over the two sheets – you ought to get 18-20 altogether. Plunge your finger in a little water and tenderly search any tops on top of the balls. Prepare for 30-35 mins, trading the plate over after 20 mins. The choux buns ought to be puffed up and fresh when cooked. Leave to cool totally.

4. To make the filling, beat the cream with the bread roll spread and flavors in a large bowl using an electric speed until delicately whipped.

5. For the caramel sauce, tip the sugar into a pot set over a medium heat, add 6 tbsp. water and cook until the sugar has broken up. Turn up the heat marginally and stew, whirling the dish sporadically until brilliant (doesn't mix or the sugar will take shape). Eliminate from the heat, add the spread and twirl the skillet until the margarine has liquefied and joined with the syrup. Immediately beat in the cream, vanilla, cinnamon, blended zest and a spot of ocean salt. Leave to cool somewhat.

6. Slice each chilled choux bun off the middle through the center. Spoon the filling into a channeling pack, clip off the end and line over the bases of the buns. Sandwich these with the tops, at that point mastermind in a generally 27cm round wreath shape on a large serving plate or board. Shower done with the caramel sauce, at that point disperse over the disintegrated rolls and gold sprinkles, if using. Best eaten immediately. Will keep chilled for up to 24 hrs.

7. Formula tip

8. In case you're in a rush, you can utilize shop-purchased dulce de leche as opposed to making the caramel sauce. Basically warm it over a low heat to release, and add a decent touch of ocean salt prior to sprinkling it over the wreath.

23. Elderflower sorbet

Prep: 30 min| Plus at least 1 hr. infusing and 6 hrs. freezing| Easy | Serves 8-10

Ingredients

- 20 heads of elderflower, newly picked
- 300g caster sugar
- 2 lemons, divided and squeezed (save the parts)

Strategy

- Pick elderflowers with perfect, smooth white petals, cutting the tail not long before the blossoms fan out. Put in a large skillet with the sugar and 550ml water, the lemon juice and the squeezed parts of the lemons. Bring to a delicate stew, at that point turn off the heat and leave to mix (and the sugar to break down) for at any rate 1 hr. or up to 5 hrs.
- Line a large strainer with muslin and set over a bowl or dish. Strain the combination and dispose of the blossom heads and lemons. Fill a freezable holder (ideally one with a top) and freeze for 2-3 hrs. until semi-frozen.

- Scratch the semi-frozen combination into a food processor or blender and barrage to separate the chunks of ice – you may have to scratch down the sides a couple of times. Set the sorbet back in the compartment and freeze for another 1-2 hrs.
- Rehash this cycle another a few times. The more occasions you mix the sorbet, the smoother it will be. Will keep frozen for as long as a quarter of a year. To serve, eliminate from the cooler and leave to represent 5 mins prior to scooping.
- Formula TIPS
- Fill in AS AN APERITIF
- Make an aperitif with elderflower sorbet by placing a scoop into a glass and pouring over an injection of gin. Kids can enjoy it with lemonade poured over all things considered.

Conclusion

Hope you liked all recipes in this book. Desserts like pumpkin pie or dull chocolate contain rich wellsprings of entire food sources that give essential nutrients, fiber, and cell reinforcements to your diet. These can easily be prepared and are beneficial for beginners.

CPSIA information can be obtained
at www.ICGtesting.com
Printed in the USA
BVHW090952030621
608731BV00011B/2326